Also by Corey Hamilton

Keep Left
Society's Grip
Exit Is A Safe Place
No One Shall Be Spared
Open Up
Mash Notes
Mash Notes: vol 2
Too Personal
Lonely Night Songs
2 Days
Unhyped
Time Marches On
Thirty Three
VI
What If?
Magic Bus
How I Remember It
Cease & Desist
Sensible Shoes
Do Not Ever Have Any Good Ideas
DNA
I Am NOT With The Band
Wedge Politics
My Side Project
Modus Vivendi

SHORT TALES & MUSINGS FROM A NEVER WAS

Copyright © 2025 Corey Hamilton

All rights reserved. No part of this book may be reproduced or transmitted in any form or by any means, graphic, mechanical or electronic, including photocopying and recording, or by any information storage or retrieval system without written permission from the publisher, except for brief passages quoted in review.

Hamilton, Corey

Short Tales & Musings From A Never Was / Corey Hamilton.

Prose/Essays

ISBN 978-1-926623-17-7

Writing, book layout and design by Corey Hamilton © 2025

Front cover photograph by Corey Hamilton © 1997

Author photo on back cover by Karlie Marrazzo © 2025
For more information on Karlie Marrazzo see below:
Instagram: @figliadifoto
Website: https://blahnewsorg.wordpress.com/

First Printing

www.dramaticsituations.com

SHORT TALES & MUSINGS FROM A NEVER WAS

Corey Hamilton

SHORT TALES & MUSINGS FROM A NEVER WAS

Hello! My name is Corey and I would like to welcome you to my latest book. I am alternating between some of my favourite essays by me and anecdotes about music by me too. The essays cover a range of topics and the music anecdotes touch on buying records & merchandise, cover art, live shows and family members dealing with me and my various music exploits.

Now for some FYI type information, I will use only the initials of my friends and full names of band members that you the reader may find interesting. Your guess is as good as mine as to why I name drop people and others I leave in the dust.

Also, I went to a great many shows and met an even greater number of music fans, musicians, promoters, etc. I'm trying to keep this book of mine as positive as possible so if I had a falling out with music fans, musicians, promoters, etc I'd leave those stories out altogether. If they are disappointed by me leaving them out of my book then they can damn well go off and write their own book. April 2021, do you see me? April of 2021 was when a lot, and I mean A LOT of things went sideways in my life.

This is the time to begin, so please fasten your seatbelts, put your trays in the upright position and keep your arms inside the windows, you don't want to lose anything important.

Huge thanks go out to my lovely wife, Jennifer (www.provokingdrama.com) & my stellar editor, Scott (I take full responsibility if there are still errors in this book after publication).

Supporters like Kenneth, Ben, Clint, Eric & Karlie, Spyder, Mike, Paddy, Phil & Rylan make this wee little book more fun to write.

3:08 am Friday, April 19th, 2024.

FRIEND AND FOE

There are reasons why I can't buy what some "friends" are selling and why I don't care if they buy what I'm selling either. I was raised in and around a conservative family. I was raised in a conservative Christian family to be exact. Although they were and are conservative Christians they made sure that my siblings and I listened to the best of our abilities and came up with our own unfettered opinions. In addition to making up our own minds they made sure that we lived with said opinions too. They may not have liked the liberal paths that my siblings and I chose to walk down, but they loved and cared for us anyway. Friends, well they are a completely different matter altogether.

I was going to name names of political figures who are right leaning but most of you will already know the players in this game. I never had too much of a problem with the right until a few years ago. I did rail and rally the troops against such "sink or swim" or "every man for himself" attitudes but now unfortunately, I feel like it's a fool's errand. Mainly because the right (and the left too) have dug in their heels and won't listen first and debate second.

It just seems like the right wing "leaders" have turned out to be narcissistic, partisan egomaniacs. Spewing their hatred on "social" media platforms all the while lifting from the playbooks of dictators from the early and mid 20th century. This scares me just as much as it angers me. Herein lies my personal dilemma. I have tried my best to listen and debate but right wing friends insist on name calling and shouting me down. All the while supporting their narcissistic fear mongering leaders. I cannot and will not go down your path. I will do my best to listen to the news and make up my mind but the people who I once called friends I will cut off from now on.

The dilemma I am having is cutting someone off in the first place. I find cutting someone off almost as distasteful as being called names by people who refuse to listen to others with dissenting views. As well as this, they refuse to listen to themselves at how eerily similar this sounds like 1930's and 40s rhetoric.

Luckily most, if not all, of my immediate family are open to listening and debating instead of name-calling and shouting down dissenting viewpoints to their own. Besides that they are my family and as long as they don't hurt me or anyone else then I can live with that. However I will not live with "friends" or people that I keep at an arm's length. I will not live with "friends" who vote for and/or support these political viewpoints and figures. People like this are enabling the right to continue this hatred by regurgitating their rhetoric and even by voting for them too.

These reasons keep me awake at night and keep me away from the trolling conservatives. Simply put, I don't have the moral compass to follow them or the moral currency to afford their insensitive, vitriolic and often sexist, racist rants. Call me judgmental if you wish and I can live with that label. I can even live with this sort of ranting from my family too. But for my own sanity and self-preservation I can't live with these so-called "friends" otherwise known as foes. I call them foes because instead of listening and debating, they name call and argue, neither of which help to diffuse the current loud angry political climate. In fact it hinders and intensifies the daily-shouting matches in the news, the circle of politics, the workplace, all of the "social" media platforms. Not only that but it makes my blood boil and my heart ache, not race, but ache. My heart aches for having to make myself just as insensitive as my former friends now foes.

MY PARENTS VS THE POLICE AND VAN HALEN AND TALKING HEADS

My parents were pretty much gatekeepers for me attending live music shows or not prior to 1986 or 87. I missed many good shows and these are two examples of great shows that I missed because of my parents gatekeeping. Looking back on it, it's in a way sad and funny. Mostly funny though.

I believe that in the late spring of 1983 I heard that The Police were coming to Edmonton (if I'm not mistaken the Thompson Twins opening) in August of 1983. At this point I wasn't even a teenager but I had a paper route, so money was not an issue with me. From about 14 to 18 I had multiple paper routes and I had a part time job at the warehouse my Dad worked at too.

I wasn't even 12 when The Police came in 1983. So I offered to buy my Mom, Dad and I tickets to the August 1983 Police show. Unfortunately they turned me down. It was a bit confusing for me because my Mom and I both liked The Police, my Dad not so much. Probably the concert experience was nixed because chaperoning an 11-year-old to a rock concert at the Edmonton Coliseum was a wee bit too much. Oh well.

In late 1983 or early 1984 a few people I knew at school were going to the April 1984 Van Halen show. My parents would usually say that I could go out to events if they knew the people I was going with. So I had that going for me because my parents knew a few people I wanted to go with.

Oddly enough my Mom wanted to hear the music first before she made her decision. So instead of playing the 1984 tile track or "Jump" which after hearing my mother would have most likely let me go. In my opinion the songs "Jump" & "1984" were not good representations of Van Halen's music. Oh no, I had to play something that was a better representation of Van Halen's music. So I picked track 1 on Side 2 of "1984" which, unfortunately for me, was "Hot For The Teacher" and right when Diamond Dave grunted loudly my Mom shouted, "That's disgustingyou're not going to go to that!" Crap. I'm an idiot.

Rarely did my mother or father watch music videos with me. One day in the mid to late 80s though my father did just that. The first video my Dad watched with me was Bad Brains, "I Against I" and soon after the song started he yelled, "For Christ's sake Corey, turn that off!!!" Another occasion had my father sit through the whole Anthrax video of, "Who Cares Wins" which is about homelessness in the USA. The music was definitely NOT my father's cup of tea but the message must have struck a chord for after the video had ended, my father said out loud, "That video was very sobering." Well put Dad, well put.

Back to the early '80s my family piled into the car for a getaway at either the farm in Manitoba or the lake lot in Saskatchewan. I don't remember which. At this time my Mom was a heavy smoker (which props to her she quit cold turkey years later) and myself and my 2 younger siblings were more than a handful for my Mom and Dad.

This one fateful evening my Mom and two siblings were fast asleep while my Dad drove on through the dark night. To help him stay up he had the radio on an AM station. It was odd that my Dad had the radio tuned to a Pop hits station because he liked '50s Rock, Country, Blues and Bluegrass. That was it. No pop, no jazz, no classical, nothing besides the 4 mentioned here.

Suddenly the radio started playing "Once In A Lifetime" by the Talking Heads and my father, who probably was stressed out to the max and white knuckling to keep from falling asleep. By the chorus, my father suddenly shouted, "WHAT IS THIS?!!" And so folks, this is how I became a massive Talking Heads fan.

I may have missed out on some shows but these memories still mean a great deal to me. Mainly because they show sides of my parents that make me smile to this day. Thanks and love Mom & Dad!

DEAD MAN CROSSING

So I just slowly crossed a marked crosswalk with my right arm outstretched, caution lights blinking, making eye contact with all of the drivers in the broad 1pm daylight and you guessed it, I was nearly hit by a car blowing through the intersection and coming close to killing me again. Believe it or not this happens to me on average twice a week in the fine city of Edmonton, Alberta, Canada. I'm getting sick and tired of this constantly occurring to me and hearing about it happening to fellow pedestrians I know too.

In not so recent memory I think that out of all of the major cities that I have visited and walked around in, Edmonton and area has some of the worst drivers in Canada. In recent memory I have visited and been a pedestrian in and around the Los Angeles area as well as in and around the Phoenix area too. And as far as I can tell Edmonton still takes the cake for car driver/pedestrian interactions.

I hear fairly often from Edmonton drivers complaining that the drivers in Montreal and Regina are way worse than Edmonton drivers. Speaking from personal experience, these Edmonton drivers are DEAD WRONG. So wrong in fact that pedestrian fatalities spiked in 2007 (13 deaths) went down for a few years and spiked again in 2015 (12 deaths) and at the time of me composing this essay Edmonton will be headed for another spike.

This has been going on for a number of years. I remember at one infamous crosswalk I had been interviewed by the CBC Television on this very topic. They interviewed me because they asked me and I informed them that I had been hit once there as well as nearly hit numerous times there too. I explained that drivers should learn to slow down, because if they kill me then not only do they ruin my life but they ruin all of my family and friends lives too. Not only this but the driver will have the fact that they were responsible for my death and ruin their own life too.

Little did I know that many of my friends watch CBC Television and little did I know that a "gentleman" after watching CBC television would contact me through my website. Apparently he took time out of his busy schedule to ask me for an interview and my phone number. Naturally I declined on giving him my phone number and told him in no uncertain terms that I stood behind my quotes on the CBC. So then he took even more time out of his busy schedule to send me a veiled threat on my life. Telling me that I should watch myself because the next time I'm out walking I may very well get killed by a driver. I guess he missed the point of my whole interview, in that nearly getting killed by a driver already happens on a regular basis.

I think that part of the problem is that drivers see pedestrians as a huge pain in the rump. No matter what the driver thinks of pedestrians, the fact remains that whether a pedestrian is in the right of way or not, a driver in their vehicle still has a far better chance of killing the pedestrian than the other way around.

Another part of the problem is that after a pedestrian is hurt or even killed the driver essentially gets a slap on the wrist, if that. A case in point is when a 19-year-old driver killed local musician David Finkleman while he crossed the street in a marked crosswalk where he even had the right of way. The Crown Prosecutor and defense jointly submitted a sentence of a two-month driving prohibition and a $2000 fine. Apparently the teenage driver responsible for Finkleman's death, at the time was a university student, had left school, and was admitted to Alberta Hospital following the collision. This will sound extremely callous towards the young driver but, honestly, I would take a mental institution, a two-month prohibition on driving and a $2000 fine over a morgue any day of the week. Not only is this a slap on the wrist but the driver just ruined Finkleman's life, his family and friend's lives as well as their own life too. So forgive me if I don't shed a tear for the driver responsible for Finkleman's death.

By the way, not only do pedestrians not paying attention while walking and or crossing on the streets drive drivers bonkers but they drive me bonkers too. They give a responsible pedestrian such as myself a bad name, but that's for another essay. To the pedestrians out there who jaywalk or generally don't pay attention, stop it and actually pay attention to your surroundings. To all of the drivers out there who speed and/or generally don't pay attention, stop it and actually pay attention to your surroundings. With all of this in mind the fact remains that a driver in a car will kill a pedestrian and not the other way around.

MY MATERNAL GRANDPARENTS & MY MUSIC CHOICES

Sometime in the summer of 1986 (probably late summer) my wonderful maternal Grandfather took me for the first time to The Attic in Calgary (or one of the earlier times while they lived in Calgary). My youngest sibling was probably at a soccer tournament. They played in tournaments across western Canada but usually, next to Edmonton, Calgary was the most.

So Grandpa and I at some point when we had free time he drove me to The Attic. Him and I went up what seemed like several flights of stairs and Grandpa just wandered around in the small store while I bought a bunch of records. When we got home Grandpa told my Mom and Grandma that the store reminded him of an opium den. Grandpa served in WWI & Korea so he was probably knowledgeable on the topic of opium dens.

I remember only 2 records I purchased that day (most likely I bought more but I only remember the 2 records) because they were the only two Grandpa took interest in. The first was "Living Heck" by Edmonton's mighty Euthanasia. Grandpa thought that the lyrics to "Mama's On Bass" were hilarious.

The second he took interest in was "Not A Pretty Sight" by Vancouver's Death Sentence. Grandpa liked the anti-Nazi artwork but the lyrics to the song "Feel Fucked" made him laugh hysterically and blurt out to my Mom and Grandma, "Hey honey, this guy says he wants to fuck you in the ass!" Grandpa continued with his laughter while my Mom and Grandma were NOT impressed at all. I wanted to crawl into a hole. To this day I still have those records because my rad Grandpa let me buy them! Thanks Grandpa!

Another time, probably summer in Calgary again but this time 1988. I went to a show in Calgary at a venue that I can't remember the name of. I attended a lot of gigs in Calgary between 1986 and 1988. The show in question was Beyond Possession (Calgary thrash/ hardcore/skate rock legends) with Joker (metal from Balzac/Calgary) and another band I can't remember the name of opening. Joker played second though. During Joker's set they announced that they had a new cassette coming out soon. I made a mental note that I must get myself one. Then Beyond Possession played and destroyed the place. So much fun! My father was supposed to pick me up at midnight but for some reason he was super late. When my father arrived he was fuming because I mixed up the quadrants and he ended up on the other side of Calgary! Oops! Sorry Dad.

Back in Edmonton I asked my maternal grandmother if she could get me the Joker cassette if I mailed her the money. She said of course and went to, you guessed it, The Attic. A week or two later Grandma called to make sure that she purchased the correct tape for me. She also said that the staff were so impressed that a grandmother went up all those flights of stairs and all that trouble just to buy her grandson (me) a Joker cassette that they gave her a bunch of free stickers to give to me! Awesome! Thanks Grandma!

So tip your hat to the coolest grandparents in Calgary! Grandma passed away in 2008 and Grandpa passed away in 2009 but I am so lucky that they both lived well into my 30s. Thanks again Grandma and Grandpa!

RETAIL CLERK BLUES

In most cases working in retail you make minimum wage and deal with maximum customer rudeness. I have worked in retail for minimum wage for close to 20 years and it never ceases to amaze me how poorly treated I am by customers as well as management. This is, in my opinion, only the tip of the iceberg with the amount of abuse one takes by working in retail.
It doesn't seem to matter what sort of retail business one is working in, the majority of customers are quite nice to deal with. It is just that the minority who make working retail/customer service work one of the most miserable jobs one can enlist in at any age. I have worked at comic stores, camera stores, record stores, candy stores, dry cleaners, screen printers, pizza call centres, etc. Unfortunately there are a select few who believe that they are entitled to treat you poorly because you work for minimum wage in customer service/retail.

I started in retail at age 16 and I'm fast approaching age 50 and however much I enjoy working in a retail job the few who are jerks make me want to jump in front of a fast moving train. Jumping in front of a fast moving train may seem like a viable option but it isn't. I believe that the people who act like I am dog crap on their shoes either have no point of reference how trying working in retail can be or they just don't care. The latter is not so easily solved but the former is.

I believe that if all people worked in retail for longer than a few weeks then maybe these entitled jerks would learn to treat customer service representatives with more respect. I believe that it should be mandatory that once one turns 18 that one must work at a retail job for minimum wage for 2 years. Just like what some countries do for conscription should be done for the customer service/retail sector.

I would go even a step further. That is to say that if you have been out of the lowly retail minimum wage job for longer than 10 years then you MUST go back and work another 2 years in the field at minimum wage. Just as a reminder as well as a nudge to be more humble when treating the minimum wage, retail worker.

I would also like to point out that for the most part the people, like me, who serve you in this line of work are emotional beings and get a bee in their bonnet once in a while too. Just like the ignorant minority of customers reciprocate the same disrespectful behavior to us. However unfortunate this is it is inevitable that it will bleed onto the customers and back onto the retail clerks. Whatever you may believe it's which came first, chicken or the egg scenario.

So the next time you are one of the rude minority of customers who decide to kick the cat (the cat being we the retail clerks) try to remember that we are human too and it is a foregone conclusion that we'll remember your ignorance long after the dust has settled. Yes, retail workers can be rude but the cumulative effect of rude customers takes its toll on us. We will burn out far quicker than it takes to train another person to replace us to deal with this sort of hostility for such lousy wages.

I believe that if customers understood and were empathetic as to how bad this job can get then maybe people like myself would stay longer and wouldn't have to vent like this as often if at all.

MUSINGS ABOUT MY GRANDPA HAMILTON

William Ronald Hamilton was born on January 19th, 1915 in Rossburn, Manitoba. To family and friends he was known as "Ron" due to the fact that his first and middle name were mistakenly reversed on his birth certificate. I knew him as Grandpa Hamilton, my father's father. Grandpa Hamilton and his wife, Mary Black were two of the most important people in my life. My reasoning behind this will follow.

One of the earliest memories I have involving my Grandfather is from when I was five or six. I was playing with some toys, as were my two sisters, in the living room of my Grandparent's farmhouse in Rossburn. Suddenly my Aunt Judy, the youngest of my father's four sib- lings, came running through the living room screaming to call the hospital. Apparently my Grandfather got bucked off of the horse he and my Aunt owned. He ended up getting the wind knocked out of him and breaking a few ribs. Even though he healed okay, it was quite a scare for everyone involved.

This last incident happened on one of the many summers my family and I spent at the farm. We tried to spend as much time with my Grandparents because around 1976 my Grandfather was diagnosed with cancer. No one admitted it at the time, but in the back of our heads, we thought Grandpa may lose the battle. So it may have been an unconscious decision to spend as much time with him as possible. The fact that almost everyone over the age of 60 on my father's side of the family has had or died from cancer was not reassuring.

For me personally most of my memories of Grandpa were good. I used to wake up early all of the time at the farm when I was younger and dress as soon as I could and wait for Grandpa to say, "Let's go for a walk." We would walk for a while around his farm until he figured that it was time for breakfast. Almost always Grandpa would start a food fight. This usually meant more work for Grandma. My Grandpa was a very demanding man, but Grandma always put up with it. In addition to Grandpa being demanding, so was I, and to a certain degree I still am. My mother feels that I got this trait from him. My mother and Grandpa locked horns on many occasions, but that's for another essay.

I understand that this is, for the most part, not very organized, but I believe that memories are almost never organized. With that in mind, I will go back to those early morning walks with Grandpa. He never said much unless I asked him a question. I remember once when I was about 17 I wondered aloud which Prime Minister candidate I would vote for when I was 18. Grandpa said, "It's too big." I didn't understand. He elaborated, explaining that things really don't change that much when they are that big. He also said that I should worry more about it at a local level and let the chips fall where they may federally. I thought this was quite profound for just a "rural redneck." There were also other bits of food for thought, like: don't complain, work it out and live one day at a time. Granted they weren't the most original pieces of information but they meant, and still do mean, a lot to me.

Grandpa taught me to be honest, fair, realistic and to try and always have fun. He never drank alcohol, did drugs, swear and quit smoking a few years before my parents were married.

Fun was almost mandatory with Grandpa around. Like afore-mentioned food fights, there were water fights and loads of practical jokes. Let me set up a scene for you: my grandparents had lots of animals like cows, horses and even a goat. The most common animals were cats, and boy, were they wild. I was about 14 and Grandpa, Dad and I were watching the cats and kittens eat the scraps of food I had put out for them. The largest cat had its back to me while it was eating and Grandpa told me to pick it up. Luckily it was winter and I had my big leather gloves on because that cat, which was not domesticated, would have torn my hands to pieces. As it was, I ended up with perforated gloves. Grandpa and Dad laughed heartily. I laughed hesitantly.

It is hard to sum up what Grandpa meant to me with all of the fading memories, but I will try my best to explain further. There was a bit of a generation gap between us. My almost severe interest in judo, hockey, art, poetry and music stirred almost nothing in my Grandpa. Even when I went through my punk rock phase and other childish rebelliousness, Grandpa (and even Grandma, which is why she is still so important to me) never made fun of me or were never disrespectful to me, unlike some of my family, close or distant. There was one incident where Grandpa hit me extremely hard. Looking back, I hold no grudges because I did something he told me not to do. I told my Dad this and he was shocked. Dad was scared to tell me because he thought it may skew my opinion of him, but Grandpa was always stressed out and very intense. This is probably because he had to support five kids and a wife on a shoestring budget. The level of intensity was so bad that Dad could hardly wait to graduate from high school so he could move out. Dad went on to say that as intimidating as his six foot one, two hundred and thirty pound father was, he never raised a hand to his children. I still see Grandpa as a sometimes serious, big teddy bear.

Of all of the differences between Grandpa and myself we had one thing in common. We loved baseball. So almost every summer when the whole family gathered at the farm, we would always play some ball in the farmyard. My fondest memory was Grandpa hitting an underhand pitch so hard that it went from one end of the yard to the other and even cleared the roof of the barn. At 74, Grandpa couldn't run very well but this time he didn't need to.

This was the second last time I saw Grandpa before I saw him in the hospital. I will not go into my feelings about seeing him naked except for a special undergarment so he could urinate, for the cancer was eating his body. I will try to forget how much weight he lost in the last months of his life and the pain and the open sores and the chemotherapy. Hearing the stories of his pain, hallucinations and going from 230 pounds to 150 pounds in a span of a couple of months. This has caused my views to be extremely polarized so that if I had to choose between cancer or A.I.D.S. to die from, I would choose A.I.D.S. in a second. I will block it all out by thinking about that rocket of a baseball he hit landing somewhere in the pasture behind the barn.

William Ronald Hamilton died March 12, 1990, losing a 13 year battle to cancer. My only regret about Grandpa and my relationship is that in our final meeting in the hospital in early 1990, I never told him that I loved him. It took me almost four years to deal with his death, I just hope that he somehow knows that I loved him, still do love him and that I miss him very much.

ANTIFA-CTS

I am in no way being sarcastic when I say that Black Metal music and lyrics are indeed art. Thought provoking art no less. Now as to whether it is lowbrow art or highbrow art is for you to decide.

Unfortunately some Black Metal artists' lyrics in question make some people, myself included, really uncomfortable. I can deal with atheism but some people can't. What myself, and a large portion of the general public (some of them are even Metal fans themselves) have an even bigger problem with are the NSBM (National Socialist Black Metal) lyrics dealing with racism, Satanism, Nazism and fascism in general.

I never really cared too much until some of these bands' music/lyrics seemed to be used for a sort of call to arms. A call to arms to burn churches, discriminate against non-whites and homosexuals and in some extreme cases to bring about a societal and racial war.

Black Metal and National Socialist Black Metal imagery is thought provoking enough to put a lot of people off. A non-Black Metal Example is Slayer's logo with the Falcon and sword. NSBM band Abgeneight's logo is far from subtle, incorporating an Aryan Nations logo in their name. Now combine the above imagery with racist and/or fascist lyrics and it all makes it hard to swallow for many people inside and outside of the Black Metal scene. Especially when it seems like, lyrically or otherwise, many Black Metal bands are NOT this way.

Some BM bands claim that these sort of racist and fascist lyrics are just sarcasm or that they are being ironic. Unfortunately some people will NEVER pick up on the nuances of said lyrics. I've read some lyrics by Taake, Horna, Marduk, Watain and Peste Noire and all of them seem to defend themselves in a similar fashion. Hoest of Taake a few years back performed in Germany with a swastika on his chest. Not only is this illegal in Germany but it is insensitive to the survivors and victims of the Holocaust and other despicable acts by Hitler. Hoest told his detractors that he was just trying to provoke a response and that they could, "Go suck a Muslim."

Provoking a response is fine but Hoest should have known what he was getting into by wearing a swastika in Germany. Unfortunately by telling someone to, "Go suck a Muslim" it is the equivalent of a 6 year old saying, "I know you are but what am I?" when the 6 year old is insulted in the schoolyard at recess.

I also found the excuse that Taake performed in Tel Aviv pretty lame. It's like when a white person is accused of being racist and they defensively respond by saying that they have a black friend. I was also wondering that since performing in Tel Aviv proves that you don't hate Jews then would Taake perform in Gaza or the West Bank to prove that they don't hate Muslims? I guess that time will only tell.

I have also read that NSBM bands say that they can't control their fans and that they are just creating and releasing confrontational art. Well that's a great way to wash your hands of some of your overzealous fans burning churches or performing racist acts of violence. Again, it's a weak defense by NSBM bands that makes them dog-whistlers at best and gas-lighters at worst. I'd like to point something else out here that not all BM fans will get the sarcasm, irony or the inside joke that BM bands are not Nazis. When growing up I listened to a lot of punk rock and hardcore and I remember seeing at a very young age the Sex Pistols wearing swastika-clad shirts. I hardly understood that they were being ironic, but then again I was barely a teenager. The same goes for songs like Chanel 3's "I Got a Gun" or the "Dead Kennedys" band name. Until it was all explained to me at an older age it all went right over my head.

So what if Peste Noire meant no harm with his Black Face "art"? I can safely speak for my black friends when I say that Black Face is horribly racist. No matter how you want to spin it, it is racist and in some cases, even to me, is terrifying. Just to clear it up Black Face is representative of the whites being racist and oppressing the already oppressed non-whites. I also find it horrifying that in 2019 there are still white people who think that this sort of crap is OK. Especially when mass shootings in Christchurch, New Zealand and the incident in Charlottesville, North Carolina are becoming more and more commonplace. The sort of implicit incitement of the lowest common denominator of Black Metal fans is totally irresponsible. Beyond that it is totally criminal that any bands, including Black Metal bands, can get away with this dog whistling.

Most Black Metal bands also claim to be different from the masses with their art. They even claim that their corpse paint is unique but unfortunately to a layman's eye such as mine, I can't tell the difference between a non-fascist song from a NSBM song or even Horna's corpse paint from shitty KISS's shitty makeup either.

I find the corpse paint thing hilarious whereas a lot of Black Metal bands have no sense of humour about it or for that matter, much of a sense of humour at all. Just ask a Black Metal band or some diehard fans what they think of the New Zealand movie "Deathgasm" and you'll see how funny they find it. I find Black Metal's lack of humour frustrating because they can make fun of you, but don't make fun of their uniforms.

A good portion of Black Metal's humour is directed at anyone who wants a safe space at a show. I have been to a great deal of shows with no safe spaces at all and at one said show I ended up going home with a sprained wrist and a minor stab wound in my lower back. Though I knew what I was getting into because I was up front at most of the show. Some people would like to enjoy the show without getting a sprained wrist or a minor stab wound. In my opinion safe spaces and non-safe spaces are both equally as valuable.

There is also a certain amount of hypocrisy involved with BM & NSBM bands alike when they are just trying to put out provoking or confrontational music but don't want any restrictions on their art. The hypocrisy is that if you don't want your art restricted then you can't expect to have restrictions put on people's reactions to your art. Whether that is rave reviews of your albums and live shows or Antifa protesting in front of the venues where you're performing. You made your bed now you can sleep in it. I don't agree with protesting in front of venues myself but I don't blame Antifa for their actions against NSBM shows.

I think that if all that happens to you is a few protestors or a show being canceled then consider yourself lucky. It is surprising that an individual or individuals don't take matters into their own hands and silence you. Like someone may have silenced Stuart Donaldson of the popular white supremacist band Skrewdriver. Reportedly a potential factor in his death in a car crash was that it appeared as if someone tampered with his shocks as well as placed a nail in one of his car's rear tires.

My Grandfather, who fought Nazis in World War 2, would be aghast that fascism is taking root not just in Canada but now the rest of the world. I'm aghast too since the Nazi/fascist playbook never ended well for anyone but especially for the Nazi fascists. The prime example of this was one evening on the evening of June 30th, 1934 called "The Night of the Long Knives." Which was early on in Hitler's reign of terror and did not go so well for the uniform wearing Brown Shirts. So it didn't go well for people in uniforms and it didn't fare much better for people not in uniforms either. It didn't go well for Jews, non-whites, homosexuals, and people with disabilities or even antisocial people either. What evidence do you have that leaders of any fascist regime would spare a bunch of people with long hair, piercings and tattoos? People like us (Punks and Metalheads alike) would most likely be some of the first to go because we are all (like Black Metal and NSBM bands think) quite different from the masses. Maybe Black Metal bands look like each other but in most cases we look completely different from the masses.

Back in the 1920s Hitler co-opted the real socialist party and their name and eventually renamed it the Nazi Party. He kept the socialist moniker to appeal to the lower classes and the disenfranchised, It would appear that NSBM bands are taking a page from Hitler's playbook, again. Keep the Socialist title to make your vitriol sound more palatable to the masses.

You'd hope that my essay would provoke a few NSBM bands and their fans to read a few history books. You'd also hope that the Black Metal bands and their fans would agree with my provoking essay and show the NSBM bands and their fans the error of their ways. It's not a stretch to say that I would like to be on the right side of history, something NSBM bands and their fans are not and will not be. Realistically this is a long shot and I know that I'm opening myself up to an attack from some Black Metal bands and their fans. But unlike a lot of Black Metal & National Socialist Black Metal bands and their fans I can sleep in the bed that I made.

"Noutajan kutsu" by HORNA

Kun kellot eivät enää saata hautajaisia
Kun talot myrkytetyt tarjoavat kuolemaa
Kun ystävien kanssa aamiaisen syötyään
Illallisen jakaa enää kirjo esi-isien
Kun kylät eivät ota vastaan muukalaisia
Kun hylättyä tietä suru yksin vaeltaa
Kun rauniouden suojaa ei etsi yksikään
Ja tervetullut on vain muisto entisten
Noutajan kutsu...
Kun ei arkunkantajaksi suostu oma perhekkään
Kun yksin vuoteen omaksi jää viimehetkinään
Kun herramme saa vihdoin todistaa
Juudean kansan tuhoa ja kuolemaa
Noutajan kutsu...
Kuolaman tanssi Tanssi viimeinen
Kuoleman tanssi Tanssi hurmeinen

(Translated to English)

"Invitation To Retrieve"

When watches no longer serve as funeral
When houses are poisoned offer death
After having breakfast with friends
Dinner divides anymore into a spectrum of ancestors
When villages do not accept strangers
When an abandoned road grieved alone wanders
No one is looking for the ruin protection
And welcome is just the memory of the former
Invitator Invitation...
When you do not agree with your family as a recruiter
When alone the bed remains your last moment
When our Lord can finally prove
The destruction and death of the Jewish people
Invitator Invitation ...
Dancing Death
The last dance
Dancing Death Dance is charming

SNFU w JR GONE WILD & KILLING TIME

The SNFU show on Saturday April 30th 1988 at 8pm was supposed to be at The Studio on 82 avenue and street but it ended up getting moved to The Polish Hall. I heard rumours that the SNFU & Beyond Possession show in January of that same year upset the community so much that they got the venue shut down, or at least to Punk shows it was shut down. I believe that it was originally a dance hall for teens that sold pop and chips to the kids hanging out there too. Great idea to give kids a place to go on the weekend instead of getting in trouble elsewhere.

So in April of 1988, after a 2 year absence of Edmonton shows and going to Calgary shows instead, I went to this zinger of a show. I bought so much merchandise including a now rare SNFU 7" that due to poverty I sold a few years back for a pretty penny. For the record, I'd rather still have the 7" single.

I loved how diverse shows were in the 80s. Killing Time a hard rock/Metal band & Jr Gone Wild a Country/Cow Punk/Rock band opening for the legendary Edmonton Punk band/Harcore band SNFU. Killing Time were great and Jr Gone Wild were even better with Mike McDonald (lead vocals & guitar) taking the piss out of the crowd for his "profanity" between songs. I thought that that took balls. I didn't really "get" them yet though so a few days later I bought their debut LP "Less Art, More Pop!" on BYO (same label as SNFU, 7 Seconds & more) and then the light went on. These guys were amazing songwriters! I'm still a Jr Gone Wild fan to this day.

SNFU were, as usual, ridiculously great and fun. I don't remember much of their set list but I do remember leaving the venue at the end with a bunch of merchandise and a huge smile on my face. Man, I really miss shows like this with multiple genres on one bill. If not for shows like these, I would never have become a fan of so much music from different genres.

FREEDOM OF SPEECH, JUST WATCH WHAT YOU SAY

For me the term, "Freedom of Speech" is and always has been a loaded phrase. I, as well as several other people in today's society, have on occasion used that phrase as a defense when we are, uh, on the defensive about something we are saying or have said.

For me "Freedom of Speech" came to the front of my radar on the evening of November 9th, 2019 when, yet again, the societal insensitive Archie Bunker of Canadian television spewed some of his ever so typical crap on air. Yes I am referring to the now infamous quote by the culturally stunted Don Cherry. Cherry typically got off the topic of Hockey and ranted that, "You people love, that come here, whatever it is, you love our way of life, you love our milk and honey. At least you could pay a couple of bucks for poppies."

Now I do NOT watch Hockey (or sports for that matter) for many reasons and this is one of the main sticking points for me. People like Don Cherry or the former coach of the Calgary Flames, Bill Peters (accused of racial slurs) are not isolated to Hockey or even pro-sports for that matter. I'm not hearing Bill Peters use the "Freedom of Speech" back up plan but Don Cherry and his troglodyte-like supporters sure did! Especially when Cherry was sent packing by the Hockey Night In Canada television station for his bullshit statement.

The fact remains that Don Cherry has been saying hockey and non-hockey related crap since he got hired. He has called out European hockey players, as well as Quebecois players, for everything under the sun from wearing protective eyewear to being soft to not wanting to fight. So it is infuriating for me that he hasn't been called out for this crap sooner. Ron Maclean (his co-host on Hockey Night In Canada) has called him out in the past but chose not to this time. Even though he offered a heartfelt apology a day later, for me it was too little too late and Maclean actually should have called out Don Cherry right after Cherry finished his xenophobic rant AND apologized. In my opinion I would have fired not just Cherry but Maclean too. That's right, the broadcaster fired Cherry 2 days later for his verbal diarrhea. As for Maclean he's safe. As for my opinion to fire Maclean too I may save it for another essay another time because I have already felt the online wrath for expressing that view.

As of today Cherry and his followers will not apologize and are still ignorantly defiant. I say ignorant because mental midgets such as these exist everywhere in modern society and commonly defend their misguided hate-filled words by shouting, "FREEDOM OF SPEECH!" I agree, everyone should be allowed to say anything that comes to their underdeveloped minds. Unfortunately for people such as Cherry, Peters, the KKK and Shane Bouchard (who stepped down as mayor of Lewiston, Maine, USA after texts were revealed in which he shared racist and sexist jokes) do not want to evolve with today's culture and/or society.

If one wants freedom of speech as a defense of their actions and/or words, then free speech. Especially if one's words are not culturally, or otherwise, accepted in today's society. If one does not like being called out for saying racist, sexist, bigoted, etc verbiage then maybe one should think before one opens their yaps. Staying with the times is called evolving. If you are ignorant and do not want to evolve or educate yourself along with society then that's YOUR problem, NOT the offended people(s) problem. That's EXACTLY how a free and open society works.

Societies evolve and you either evolve with society by educating yourself or keep your insensitive ass out of public. Online or otherwise. So yes freedom of speech still exists for the likes of Don Cherry, his acolytes and anyone else using the freedom of speech defense to defend their ignorance. Just don't forget that today's society also has freedom too, it's called accountability and today's society will indeed hold you, me or anyone else accountable. And I for one don't mind one little bit.

JOHNY BOWER LOST A FAN

This short essay on my Mom's Dad, my Grandpa, is kind of mixed up but hopefully it will make some sense by the end.

Grandpa served in the military in two wars, the Navy in World War 2 and the Army in Korea. He always had stories to tell about his life in or out of the military. I only remember one story of his being really sad. In World War 2 he served on the H.M.C.S. Sackville (the last Corvette in the Canadian Navy). The story was of a friend of his serving on the same boat as him during World War 2. His friend was responsible for firing bombs called "Hedgehogs" into the water and whenever they exploded it meant two things. The first was that a German U-Boat was hit and that the U-Boat was now sinking to the bottom of the ocean. The second was that my Grandpa's friend would start vomiting overboard into the water because he thought that that was the worst way to die, sitting at the bottom of the ocean waiting for the oxygen to run out. Overall Grandpa rarely talked about the wars and I didn't press him either. My Mom told me that once Grandpa punched a Captain in the nose and lost his stripes over it. That sounded about right because Grandpa could be pretty stubborn. Sometime after the 2 wars Grandpa met Toronto Maple Leafs great, Johnny Bower. Grandpa was a big Leafs fan so to meet a star Maple Leafs player was a highlight for him.

Grandpa had a supportive wife and they were like two peas in a pod. Grandpa and Grandma had two lovely daughters and several grandchildren and great grandchildren. In his later years Grandpa made these quirky birdhouses for the family. He quit smoking when I was born and years later he quit drinking. In August 2008 doctors found a cancerous tumor in Grandpa's throat. Then on September 14, 2008. Grandma passed away and Grandpa's stories stopped (at least it seemed that way to me). These last two events seemed to take the wind right out of Grandpa's sails. I saw him in the hospital a few times getting radiation treatment and such but the stories had ended and most of the time he slept.

On Friday April 10, 2009 Grandpa suffered a stroke and four days later, on the evening of April 14, 2009, Fred Arthur Barnard passed away, just two weeks shy of his 88th birthday.

It is times like these that I sometimes ignore my atheist side and right now I would like to think that maybe, just maybe somewhere, Grandma is having a drink and listening to Grandpa tell his stories. And although they miss us and we miss them Grandma and Grandpa are having a great old time.

CIRCLE JERKS, 7 SECONDS, WICKER MAN & KILLING TIME
JULY 2, 1988

Sometime around May or June of 1988 a friend at school asked me if I was going to the Circle Jerks and 7 Seconds show in July of the same year. I said, "of course!"

The night of the show my friends and I piled into a few cars and drove from Sherwood Park to Eastwood Hall in Edmonton. Being as how school was out for the summer and a lot of my friends from school were at the show it turned out to be like a high school reunion of sorts. I remember Killing Time and Wicker Man being decent but I was really only there for 7 Seconds and Circle Jerks were a bonus to me at the time. I liked the Circle Jerks but 7 Seconds' songwriting, ethos and image really resonated with me and still do to this day. I don't know what the pits were like for Killing Time and Wicker Man because I was at the back of the hall for them. But the pit for 7 Seconds had a decent amount of women slamming and stage diving. Which made sense with 7 Seconds' "Not Just Boys Fun" song and overall stance that women should be able to participate in Punk Rock & Hardcore.

I was right up front for 7 Seconds first song (I didn't leave the pit until their last song) and at one point Kevin Seconds (7 Seconds vocalist and primary songwriter) put the mic to me and I did a whoah whoah. Then it was my turn to stage dive. I climbed on the stage, dove and in my opinion, perfect form too. Unfortunately for me though, even though I was only 120 pounds soaking wet the crowd parted like the Red Sea and I landed on the Eastwood Hall's hardwood floors flat on my back, knocking the wind out of me in the process. I could barely breathe, then as luck would have it, a saint yelled at me, "Hey! You're J.W.'s friend! Get up!" He helped me up and when I got my wind back the fun ensued. Just no more stage diving.

Next the headliner, Circle Jerks, hit the stage and I was only in the pit for part of the first song before the violence turned me off. I went to the back again and stood with J.W. on a table for the rest of the Circle Jerks set. When Circle Jerks did the song "Wonderful" and Keith Morris (Circle Jerks vocalist and songwriter) did his whistling parts, feedback screamed through the P.A. and J.W. beside me had been struggling with headache already but with the feedback screaming they buckled over in agony. Once the feedback ended the table with a couple of people on it in front of J.W. and I collapsed. J.W. and I looked at each other and made the wise decision to get down and stand on the floor.

Soon after, maybe 2 or 3 songs into their set, Keith Morris stopped the show during mid-song to say that if the fighting didn't stop, then the Circle Jerks would stop the show and leave. Miraculously the pit from my vantage point seemed to calm down.

Merch you ask? Of Course! I bought 2 Circle Jerks shirts because they had won me over with their show and now I became a super fan. I had liked them before the show but now I LOVED them. I bought a beautiful purple and teal tie dyed 7 Seconds shirt along with it and the B.P. poster, I still have to this day.

What a wonderful summer memory from 1988, between grades 11 and 12. And to this day, this show is still my favourite show. On a side note, years later I discovered that R.L. had put on this show which is kind of cool that our paths crossed a few years before I first met them at the Ambassador. Every so often I tell R.L. that their show is still my favourite show of all time and it brings a smile to their face and mine.

MULTIPLE TAKES

So I am into watching movies a little less than listening to music even though I watched and or owned movies well before music. The first movie I saw in the theatre was a double bill of Return of The Pink Panther & Star Wars: A New Hope in 1978. Return of The Pink Panther did absolutely nothing for me, but Star Wars was another story. I loved it.

Soon after Star Wars my parents would take us out to the occasional movie like the Star Wars trilogy, Ghostbusters, Raiders of The Lost Ark, The Muppet Movie(s), Superman (1978), King Kong (1979) and among those, EVERY damn John Hughes film. Before my parents owned a VCR they would rent a Laser Disc player or a VCR and we'd watch War of The Worlds (1953), Superman 2 (1980), Indiana Jones & The Temple of Doom and EVERY damn John Hughes film. My parents (bless their hearts) would have a movie playing for myself and my 2 younger sisters monthly (it seemed more often than that but my memory is really foggy) with, you guessed it, EVERY damn John Hughes movie. Which is where I started to dislike my family's taste in films.

Even though I, by and large, disliked my family's taste in cinema, I would occasionally listen to them. Like when my mother explained to me that the old man at the end of The Muppet Movie (1979) was the legendary Orson Welles who had a hard time making movies. Later on in my teens I looked into Welles' Citizen Kane because it was considered Welles best film and the greatest film of all time. Ba, humbug! Impossible I said, until I watched it and realized why it was considered the greatest film of all time. To this day it is my favourite film. Another time this time in 1991 one of my Dad's younger brothers raved to me about the first 2 Godfather films and mentioned that part 3 was mediocre at best. Soon after I watched the first two Godfather films for the first time and was blown away how good gangster films could be. I watched numerous gangster films after that and again, was mostly disappointed. The bar was set high with Coppola's first two Godfather films.

I never liked any of John Hughes' films or Ghostbusters. I liked some of the actors in those films and a few lines but overall these seemed like cookie cutter films to me. During grade school a friend and I would rent films too. Aliens, Scanners, Videodrome, Apocalypse Now we loved but Predator we laughed our asses off at how terrible it was. Around the age of 14 I realized that I rarely liked Hollywood films so I ended up going to the local video store (by now my parents owned a VCR) and rented mainly horror films. I really gravitated to horror films and ended up watching horror almost exclusively. Occasionally I'd go see movies on my own (Tim Burton's Batman & Beetlejiuce) but yet again I was by and large disappointed.

Then 1990 happened when I met my first girlfriend. She didn't like horror films (perish the thought!!!) but knew I didn't like Hollywood films so she suggested that we go out to The Princess Theatre in Old Strathcona and watch independent and foreign films as well as renting movies. This was the best thing that happened to me in my brief film watching life. She and

I ended up going almost weekly to the Princess. Between going to The Princess Theatre and renting we saw many films there Betty Blue, Miller's Crossing, Bad Lieutenant, Being At Home With Claude, The Adjuster, Exotica, La Femme Nikita, Night On Earth, Paris Texas, Short Cuts, The Vanishing (1988), Barton Fink, Cinema Paradiso, I Love A Man In Uniform and many, many more. Up to 1992 to 1995 my opinion was set in stone and I rarely went to or watched Hollywood movies. When my first girlfriend and I went to a large commercial movie theatre she took me to Naked Lunch and Highway 61 and I took her to Apocalypse Now and Hearts of Darkness all in 1991. We would have a "bad" movie night every so often where we'd each rent a terrible film. Hers' was Roadkill and mine was Deathrace 2000 (1975) just for laughs.

After our relationship fizzled out I went to films on my own like the Star Wars prequels, Fight Club, American Pie, Eyes Wide Shut and Bone Collector all of which I didn't really care for. So for the most part I stayed away from Hollywood...again. With that in mind the few years we spent together had a long reach and I still gravitate to "artsy" movies. So back to renting horror and artsy films like Being John Malkovich, Eternal Sunshine of The Spotless Mind, Bottle Rocket, Blood Simple, Blue Velvet, Mullholland Drive, Ghost World, The Apprenticeship of Duddy Kravitz, American Splendor and more.

In 2011 I went to visit my current wife for the first time and I introduced her to my quirky movie taste and she introduced me to some Hollywood films. For the most part I liked her film suggestions but I ignored them at the time of release because of my track record with Hollywood (insert Public Enemy's song "Burn Hollywood, Burn"). She and her parents lived outside of Los Angeles and seemed to go to several movies. This makes sense when you grow up and live right beside the Hollywood movie industry centre of the world. My wife enjoyed some of my picks (some she didn't) and her parents seemed to enjoy some of my picks too. For example, one of my favourite films from 1990 was Rosencrantz & Guildenstern Are Dead. My wife's Mother seemed to enjoy it whereas she didn't seem to like Metropolis (1927). My mother and father-in-law and I watched Stanley Kubrick's Noir film from 1956 The Killing and we all enjoyed that early Kubrick effort.

I still watch a great deal of movies and I'd like to think that my mind has opened a bit more with my wife and her parents in my life. I'll give some Hollywood films a chance now whereas before I wouldn't even watch a trailer. Logan, The Big Short, Resident Evil, Collateral, some smaller films The Last Night, some horror films The Fog (1980) The Thing (1982) and coming full circle, you guessed it EVERY damn John Hughes film. Just kidding. What I meant to say is, and coming full circle, Star Wars films. One thing is for certain, my taste in cinema is still quite picky, I might give a Hollywood film a chance, I will still watch horror, foreign, independent and Star Wars films and I still don't like a single damn John Hughes' film.

MY FAVOURITE ALBUM COVERS

So when I first started buying records (I was about 12 or 13) I bought mostly what I heard but the rest of the time my purchase choices were because of a great album's cover art. U2 "War" & The Alarm "Strength" were two early examples.

I would take bi-weekly trips from Sherwood Park into Edmonton to shop at what I called affectionately "The Strip" - The Marquee on the corner of 101 Street and 107 Avenue, then Freecloud Records on the corner of 101 Street and 108 Avenue and in between was my go to source for my record purchases, Sound Connection. 3 decent record stores.

Sometime in 1985 (probably different weeks but I can't be sure) at Sound Connection on the new releases rack by the Punk Section were Two albums with artwork that shook me, one I bought instantly and the other years later. The latter was "Feast" by Würm with a naked woman holding out an orange but shot in what appears to be colour infrared film. The effect is jarring so I passed on that record for years. Würm's music on this album is amazing and I highly recommend this Chuck Dukowski and Ed Danky band.

The former album was "Bad Moon Rising" by Sonic Youth. I remember seeing the cover on the new release punk rack and saying to myself, "I have no idea who Sonic Youth are but that is the best album cover of all time and I have to buy it." From then on I was a Sonic Youth fan. So much so that I wrote them back in 1985. Their album covers were usually amazing, "Evol" & "Goo" are two that come to mind. Simple, artsy and sometimes disturbing.

Years later I soured on Sonic Youth for a few reasons but the three main ones were that I wrote them in 1985 and never received a response. Oh well. Shit happens, it was only one stamp. So I moved out of my parent's home in 1990 and I did so much mail-ordering that I was still getting my music related mail sent to my parent's home all the way up to 1993.

Including Christmas cards from Soundgarden (!) and a blue highlighter and a few singles from Shadowy Men On A Shadowy Planet but the insult was in late 1992 my parents dropped off my mail and in the batch was a postcard from Sonic Youth wanting me to give them $20 USD annually to join their fan club. That was insult number 1, insult number 2 was watching Narduar interview Sonic Youth and how poorly all four members treated him. A few years later someone (I think Narduar again) interviewed Lee Ranaldo of Sonic Youth and the interviewer brought up Sonic Youth's past bullshit and Ranaldo claimed that he didn't remember that. Maybe he doesn't remember but I think that he did and was just trying to save face.

Reason number 3 was what seemed to me to be an acrimonious divorce between two Sonic Youth members Thurston Moore and Kim Gordon. Thurston Moore apparently was having an affair. Moore and Gordon had a child together which makes their divorce extra shitty. I contend that, by and large, these famous men who have affairs only do it because they can. Even if the person comes forward to a married man to have extra marital sex the man can always say "no" but instead the males jump into bed and then a lot of the time claim that it "just happened." Yeah right.

All of this Sonic Youth drama is what caused me to sour on them. I still own a few records and listen to them frequently and to this day I still believe that "Bad Moon Rising" is the greatest album cover of all time. Now if you expect me to explain why these are my favourite album covers you're going to be disappointed. It's totally visceral and subjective, like all art is for me.

EDMONTON LIVE MUSIC CROWDS

I contend that Edmonton live music fans/crowds can either be great or absolute shitty.

I remember that a lot of the crowd that attended the Soul Asylum show in 1992 were the latter. Throwing loonies and heckling Soul Asylum so badly that the band walked off the stage early.
I remember that the crowd that attended the Today Is The Day, KEN mode, Black Tusk & Fight Amp show were the former, great. It seemed like it sold out the venue and the crowd were so enthusiastic that the bands seemed to pick up on it too. It was an Easter long weekend no less.

Another show where I felt that the Edmonton crowd were amazing was the local No Hands & Japan's Mono opening for Montreal's Fly Pan Am show. I photographed and spoke to all three bands. Mono was tough because they, for the most part, did not know much English. Same with Fly Pan Am from Montreal with their bassist being the only bilingual member, the other members seemed to only speak French. No matter, all three bands were extremely nice to my fanboy chatter.

Edmonton's No Hands were visually interesting. They all wore primary coloured raincoats with their backs to the audience for most of their set. Mono was next and they started out really

quiet and then all of a sudden a wall of sound blasted me up front and I enjoyed Mono's performance. I enjoyed their set so much that I used 2 full rolls photographing their set alone. The bassist, Tamaki Kunishi, for some reason that eludes me, is the most viewed photograph on my site. According to Google analytics it is anyway.

Fly Pan Am came on and were amazing, somehow a step up from the stellar Mono set. This show was at the original Sidetrack (RIP) and the crowd was bouncing and cheering to the beat so much that I swear that I felt the Sidetrack's floor moving to the beat of each Fly Pan Am song. The show was supposed to end at midnight but seemed to me to go well past that time. Fly Pan Am seemed to do at least 2 or 3 encores and at one point one of their guitarists came back out onto the stage and shouted into the mic, "Vive Le Edmonton!!!" As the bands and venue staff were cleaning up I went and chatted to the bilingual Fly Pan Am bassist and he was so happy that he hugged me and said that this show was the best of the whole tour.

Take that Soul Asylum hecklers. I hoped that Soul Asylum and Fly Pan Am would come back and headline their respective shows in Edmonton Again. So far neither band seems to have come back to play here. Soul Asylum, I totally get. But if Fly Pan Am ever comes back, I'll be there. Guaranteed.

MIDNIGHT OIL - TUESDAY, OCTOBER 25TH, 1988

Sometime in the summer of 1987 I bought the new album by Midnight Oil, "Diesel and Dust" who were one of my favourite bands. Midnight Oil became a favourite of mine in the summer of 1984 or 1985 when a coworker asked me for a blank tape so he could dub me a record that he thought that I'd like. That album, "10, 9, 8, 7, 6, 5, 4, 3, 2, 1, 0" Midnight Oil's 4th album from 1982. My coworker thought that I'd like it since I mainly listened to "weird music on my Walkman" or so he believed.

Soon after I bought all of Midnight Oil's previous work and current music. From their debut S/T album in 1978 to their 1984 album "Red Sails In The Sunset" and everything between. I was hooked.

So it was a no-brainer that I would be attending the Midnight Oil show in October of 1988. This was their first time headlining a show in Edmonton. Previously Midnight Oil opened for Flock of Seagulls in 1983 but that was before my time. I bought tickets in the summer of 1988 and impatiently waited for October 25th to arrive.

Somehow J.W. and myself got in the first row with C.P. and M.M. (RIP, I miss you M.M.) and the four of us stayed put for the whole show because when the lights went out the crowd surged forward and pinned the four of us right against the stage's barrier. On the other side of the barrier between it and the stage, security (as well as someone on the stage) implored us to move back to no avail. With their pleading unheaded, the show started. I enjoyed the opening acts of Yothu Yindi & Graffiti Man but I was really there only for Midnight Oil. Midnight Oil at this time were more Punk than a lot of Punk bands in the late 80s. Midnight Oil walked the walk.

The lights dimmed and the background was just the sun rising with Midnight Oil opening with a bang, the song with one of the greatest bass lines, "Progress" from their 1985 EP, "Species Deceases". The bass line from "Progress" to me, was up there with the bass lines from Jane's Addiction's "Mountain Song" and Nomeansno's "Rags and Bones". Midnight Oil never let up once during the whole show and I "sang" and "danced" my butt off. I knew every lyric of every song that they played off by heart. At some point during the show M.M. was repeatedly poking me really hard in my left shoulder (M.M. then C.P. and J.W. were all to my left side) and I yelled at M.M., "WHAT?!!" M.M. point to the space between the barrier and the stage where vocalist Peter Garrett was running back and forth smacking everyone's outstretched hand. So of course I stuck my hand out and to my surprise, Peter Garrett stopped, grabbed my hand, shook it vigorously, came close to my face and said, "Thank you!" Then he got back up on the stage and continued the rest of the show. Why on Earth was Peter Garret thanking me and for what?

After the show and the four of us got outside, M.M. claimed that every band member of Midnight Oil was watching at points during their set! I can only surmise that maybe a 16 year old in nowhere-ville, Canada who knew all of their lyrics by heart threw them for a loop. Maybe Midnight Oil expected their fans to only know their current album, "Diesel and Dust" but I'm only guessing and I will never know. Regardless, the October 1988 Midnight Oil show is still one of my all time favourite concerts I have ever attended.

THE MOHAWK RESISTANCE 30 PLUS YEARS ON

I, Corey Hamilton, acknowledge Treaty 6 territory—the ancestral and traditional territory of the Cree, Dene, Blackfoot, Saulteaux, Nakota Sioux, as well as the Métis. I acknowledge the many First Nations, Métis and Inuit whose footsteps have marked these lands for generations. I am grateful for the traditional Knowledge Keepers and Elders who are still with us today and those who have gone before us. We recognize the land as an act of reconciliation and gratitude to those whose territory we reside on or are visiting.

So on the morning of either Wednesday July 11th, 1990 or Thursday July 12th, 1990 my headspace was terrible. I came into work sad, upset, disturbed and embarrassed. Why? I had a good paying job in a warehouse (roughly $16 an hour for 40 hours a week with benefits) I had my teeth fixed, including all of my wisdom teeth yanked paid for by my benefits plan. I bought my first car, I was seeing upwards of 8 live bands a week and I was living on my own.

Why was I in such a bad state you may ask? Simple. I was the youngest and only left leaning person in the whole Edmonton branch and being white too meant that I had to listen to all of the other white (EVERYONE was white at this location) people from the branch manager bully, the warehouse manager bully and everyone else spew their racist crap concerning the media branded "Oka Crisis" in Quebec. Though it was known by supporters as "The Mohawk Resistance."

Now normally my big mouth would have opened and barked back. In this case I didn't because changing everyone's (or anyone else's minds for that matter) was a fool's errand. An example was when I brought up the internment of Japanese Canadians in World War 2 one of my coworkers stated that all is fair in love and war. I told him on no uncertain terms that there was no war in Canada and these people were Canadians too. That did not go over well. So again, I shut my yap.

If you're not familiar with the 78 day standoff that started on July 11, 1990 ending on September 26, 1990 then here's the abridged version. Back in March of 1989 a bunch of white politicians and white businessmen thought that it was a good idea to expand the Club de golf d'Oka over top of a centuries old Mohawk Tribe's burial ground.

Some people (indigenous and white) protested to the white politicians (municipal, provincial and federal) but their protests fell on deaf ears. In late June of 1990 blockades were erected by the Mohawks and other indigenous peoples from Canada and the USA but on July 11th, 1990 the mayor asked the Quebec Provincial Police Force and the RCMP to intervene. The Mohawks stood their ground and gunfire erupted after the authorities deployed tear gas and concussion grenades. The Police fell back leaving 6 police cruisers and a bulldozer behind while several people were injured and one police officer was shot and killed.

On August 8th the white Quebec premier requested military support but it was denied. Again on August 14th the RCMP were overwhelmed and they backed down. On August 20th the military were sent in. On August 29th a stand down was negotiated and on September 26th the remaining Mohawk protesters dismantled the blockades and returned to their reserve after burning some of their guns and a ceremonial tobacco burning. Some of the Mohawks felt betrayed even though the plans to expand the golf course were canceled. I can't say as I blame them for feeling betrayed. I'll clarify this later.

So all of this culminated in me keeping my yap shut and listening to every damn one of my white coworkers give their racist play by play of the whole event. They all read that terrible right wing tabloid rag, The Edmonton Sun, which by the way, promoted my coworker's racist views and banter with their bullshit take on a sad, upsetting, disturbing and embarrassing piece of Canadian history.

78 days after it had started the bigots at work found another person or persons to blame for their current woes. I went back to work with my yap shut tight and disillusioned that nothing on either side had changed. Their side, my side or for that matter the Mohawks and the politicians too. Except that the golf course expansion was scuttled.

Like I just stated, the Canadian municipal, provincial and federal governments didn't change one iota. Our current Prime Minister talks a good talk but reconciliation with the indigenous population is far from becoming a reality. With most, if not all, reserves lacking the basics like clean drinking water, sanitation and in some cases even electricity. Things that almost every other Canadian takes for granted.

As of the date that I published this the blockades continue as well as all levels of government continuing to harass, arrest the protesters or shut the blockades down all together. Just look up Wet'suwet'en protests or any other indigenous protests across Canada and you will find that many of them are still ongoing even though all levels of the Canadian government has shut them down. Sometimes even regular citizens like truckers, people who work in the oil and gas sector or outright racists like the Canadian Yellow Vest movement (which by the way is not even close to what the original Yellow Vest movement in by the way is not even close to what the original Yellow Vest movement in France is) or Sons of Odin or Proud Boys. Regular citizens? Nope. Regular racist colonizers? Yup.

That's the exact reason why I went into work 30 years ago in such a foul mood. Something inside told me that 30 years later this anniversary would drudge up the same emotions again. Being sad, upset, disturbed and embarrassed. Something told me that 30 years later on this anniversary my hopes for reconciliation would be dashed. I'm sure the Mohawk tribe and all other tribes across Canada would feel the gamut as well as betrayed too that after 30 years they're still fighting the same damn fight.

Now ask yourself, if someone didn't give you clean drinking water, sanitation, electricity, took your land away and to top it all off, decided to build a stupid golf course on your ancestor's cemetery then how would you feel and what would you do? If your answer is anything less than put up a blockade or riot or even just a peaceful protest then you are an entitled, lying, hypocrite with zero empathy and compassion for the marginalized indigenous population. Not only that, you are also part of the problem and will eventually end up on the wrong side of history.

Oh, and if you think that I'm in a bad mood after nothing has changed 30 plus years after The Mohawk Resistance, then try being a Canadian Indigenous person when nothing has changed in the 300 years after being colonized and see how you'd like it.

FUGAZI AUGUST 17TH, 1991 MACEWAN HALL CALGARY, AB

In 1991 B.B. gave me Ian MacKaye's phone number because he heard through the grapevine that Fugazi was wanting to tour Canada for the 1st time. I called and Ian confirmed this but the dates available made it near impossible to play Calgary, Edmonton and then Vancouver. I recommended he play Calgary and head to Vancouver and passed him onto W.H. W.H. had me poster and sell tickets up here.

So August rolls around and myself, A.H. and a few other friends pile into my little car and head down to Calgary. We went our separate ways soon after we arrived because I had to meet with W.H. and get him the remaining tickets and money. At the show I was setting up the Skin Barn merch table and one of the venue's management tried to squeeze me for money from the shirt sales. I diplomatically told him to fuck off because Skin Barn had barely any merch to sell and were not big rockstars. He walked away.

During Skull Buni & Skin Barn all I heard from attendees was, "are you selling any Fugazi merchandise?" Jeez, these people were dumb, did they not listen to the Fugazi song on "Repeater" called "Merchandise"? Idiots. It was so bad that Skin Barn told the audience during their set that Fugazi doesn't sell merchandise at their shows. Literally one song later a young woman asked for Fugazi merch. Ugh.

During the Fugazi set I took some pictures of them and they played a great set except that they were way too loud. Even B.B. said so the next time I ran into him in Edmonton. After the show was over I chatted with Fugazi and came home. I processed the negatives right after I got home and immediately hated the pictures and filed them away.

Flash ahead 25 years or so and I found the negatives. I emailed Ian Mackaye and he even remembered myself and W.H.! Wow! I asked him if he'd like my negatives and he said yes. So I shipped them off and the fine folks at Dischord scanned, edited and sent me the digital versions. Ian loved them so much he added them to the Fugazi live series album of the night. Anyhow, I only liked one snapshot I took from that evening though. Oh well. Oh, and contrary to popular belief, Ian and company were at times ridiculously funny.

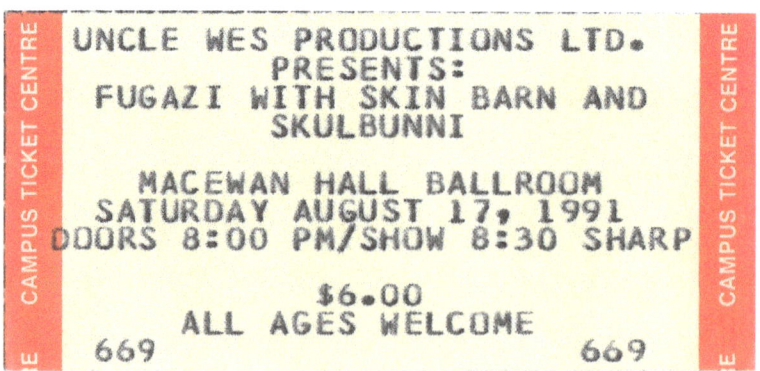

THREE DAYS IN 1988

- *PROLOGUE* -

Sometime in the summer of 1988 I was working my summer job like I had the previous 3 or 4 summers. I believe that I had already bought a ticket to Skinny Puppy in late September of 1988. I was doing my usual shipping and receiving duties when one of the local rock radio stations played an advertisement for Iggy Pop's show. I somehow convinced my Dad to hand over his credit card and promptly called BASS (a precursor  to Ticketmaster) and asked to buy a ticket to Iggy Pop. The woman informed me that I was lucky because there were only 7 tickets left. I was pretty bummed to hear that my seats were going to suck. So I asked the woman if I could buy one ticket to Iggy Pop as close to the front and centre of the stage as possible The woman on the other end of the phone replied, "A15." Which to my surprise was as close to the front and centre of the stage as one could get! Awesome!

So the Skinny Puppy and Iggy Pop tickets were mailed to me and I had to wait for their respective shows until late September. Upon closer inspection of my Skinny Puppy and Iggy Pop tickets I noticed an odd but amazing detail in the 2 tickets. Skinny Puppy was playing at the SUB Theatre (now called Myer Horowitz Theatre) on Thursday, September 29, 1988 and Iggy Pop was playing the same venue on Friday, September 30, 1988! Awesome! Two shows I was looking forward to seeing back to back at the same venue! I could hardly wait!

- *CHAPTER 1* -

The summer ended, school started again and the leaves were turning. It was mid September when I found a God & Disciples of Power poster for their October 1st show at The Chinook Theatre. I never was a fan of Disciples of Power, but God was an amazing live band. Ken Hare was a beast of a drummer and I really enjoyed Ford Pier's stage presence. Now I have 3 shows in 3 days to go to!

So the evening of Thursday September, 29 rolled around and the performance by Skinny Puppy was amazing. They were touring on my favourite Skinny Puppy album, "VivisectVI", and to this day it was the loudest show I have ever attended. The Ramones in 1990 were loud, Unsane in 1998 were loud too but not like Skinny Puppy. Although I didn't get punched in the balls for crowd surfing at Skinny Puppy like I did at the Ramones show. Unsane and Kittens in 1998 were loud too but again, not like Skinny Puppy.

I danced up front and had loads of fun. The visuals were the highlight for me because it was so loud I couldn't distinguish each song very well. It was so loud in fact that my friend's lighter was constantly being blown out by the PA whenever he tried to light his cigarette. That's how loud. Note, in 1988 one was still allowed to smoke cigarettes inside of the concert venues. I had a few drinks and was only a little tipsy but I didn't overdo the drinking because I had school the next morning.

- *CHAPTER 2* -

Friday came along and again, I took the bus into the city from Sherwood Park to the same Edmonton venue as the previous night with Skinny Puppy, just today Iggy Pop, a personal hero of mine, was performing. I bought a "Raw Power" shirt even though I really wanted a "Raw Fucking Power" shirt and skipped the first band altogether.

So myself C.P. and M.M. went to the front. I was between C.P. on my left and M.M. on my right. Iggy was touring the "Instinct" album of which I got a promotional Iggy Pop pop can from Sam The Record Man in West Edmonton Mall earlier that same year. C.P. & M.M. and myself were kind of drunk and up front when Iggy and his band were partways in their show, doing the Stooges classic, "Shake Appeal". Speaking for myself, I was not prepared in any way for Iggy's antics that evening. During the guitar solo I looked up to see Iggy flying through the air after he dove. In my head I thought, "Oh shi...." when he landed hard on my head, rolled off of me onto M'M. and then was promptly yanked back on stage.

Iggy and company continued without missing a beat. They did "I Wanna Be Your Dog", "The Passenger" and many more. At the end of the show I found another "Raw Power" tshirt so I hauled ass to the merch table to get a "Raw Fucking Power" shirt instead but unfortunately the merch table was gone for the evening. Bummer.

In the car ride home, C.P. was driving myself, M.M. and A.B. home really, I mean really slowly. All four of us were pretty drunk and very stupid for drinking and driving. Suddenly C.P. realized that they had been driving all along with the emergency brake on. Oops. Suddenly M.M. blurted out, "I just remember someone's groin in my face!" C.P. and I informed them that that was none other than shirtless Iggy's groin in their face. I don't remember much more but that we somehow got home safe and sound in the wee hours of Saturday morning. Stupid booze.

- CHAPTER 3 -

Or should I say stupid Corey with booze? Because I ended up getting loaded before the Disciples of Power & God show. By the time I had got to The Chinook Theatre via public transportation I was blotto but with a red gig poster for the show and a few bucks in my pocket to cover the door charge. Did I mention that I have no idea what the show was like because I was blotto? I don't even remember how I got home! Oops!

- EPILOGUE -

When I woke up Sunday morning after 3 days of music my head was pounding and my breath smelled like dogshit and instead of one red Disciples of Power & God gig poster, I now had one green poster and two red posters. One of the red posters had "Sacred One Dies" written in the letters of G O D and it was not my handwriting. OK. 3 shows in 3 days was the first and last time I ever did that. It was fun but I swear that my ears were ringing for a month afterwards.

A JUVENILE RESPONSE TO A JUVENILE RANT

This is my response to two Americans who criticized me several times and threatened me once on the Internet. To protect the ignorant, the female shall be called "Hosehead" & the male shall be called "Hoser".

I just thought that I would take time between my two jobs to send Hoser and Hosehead a response, even though one of you implies my mouth is open too much and the other complains about my silence. Oh well, you can't please everybody.

1 – Hosehead not wanting to "rehash old entries" is sheer laziness because I see nothing wrong with sending me the links to appropriate pages with information that could possibly change my mind. I do it all the time.

2 – As for me mocking Hosehead, yes I did, only after she called me a pet name MOCKINGLY. The only people who can call me pet names are my parents, my grandparents and my current girlfriend. Hosehead is (thankfully) none of the above.

3 – Hoser had you read the rest of my "silly hat rant" (see poem #1596 at the bottom of this diatribe) you would have read that I do NOT believe in any prophets, messiahs, Gods, devils, Heavens or Hells. To quote Hosehead, "you should have done your homework."

4 – I deleted Hosehead's response to my critique of her because it did not offer any insight to my brilliant writing skills. By the way, I delete far more comments than I let be posted and most of the time the people who I graciously let their comments grace my blog with their comments are ones I know personally. As for you two, well, need I say more?

5 – Hoser called me a coward yet he is the one who hides behind a N.R.A. card and a gun. Anybody who hides behind a gun is a coward. I have been teaching Judo for 10 years and I still don't feel the need for a gun. Oh Hoser, what's this fascination with guns? I think you must be over-compensating for a small penis or something of that nature.

6 – I respect myself first and foremost and I believe that no self respecting human being should want and/or need pity, in other words if you pity anyone it should be your sorry excuse for an insult. I started off by saying that I took this time between my two jobs to respond, my first job being practicing and the teaching of neurosurgery at one of the hospitals in this city and my second job at night is an air traffic controller at the international airport. So a few days ago three col- leagues and I were discussing your sorry ass attempt at a blog and I said that Hoser called my tattoos "derivative", my three colleagues asked in unison (the same thing I asked myself), "derivative of what?" I see that you are a graphic designer for television so I understand it might be hard to grasp the English language when you are drawing and looking at pictures all day. I will help you out, there is a book called a dictionary. In this book it has definitions of all words in the English language, for your ease I will now place the definition of "derivative" (like the poem #1596) at the bottom of this diatribe. I would suggest that before you use big words you try a dictionary first. Once you have mastered that book you may want to graduate to something called a "thesaurus", and no it is not a large, extinct reptile. It is another book, feel free to look up "thesaurus" in a dictionary if you would like. If you were trying to insult me and

my lifestyle choice for body art I would suggest a smaller word, like "dumb" (the "b" on the end is silent) I think it is safe to say you know what "dumb" means because when referring to people like you "dumb" is usually followed by "ass", which is what my American brother calls Americans (the likes of which he is embarrassed by) who fall into several stereotypes. 1: Americans who can't read 2: Right wing Americans who can't read 3: Religious right wing gun-toting wing nut Americans who can't read. So to keep a level playing field I will stereotype myself as well.

So up here in Canada in our mukluks and snowshoes all we do is hunt moose, watch hockey and drink beer, eh. We don't know anything about you savages...er...Americans and your guns and we are all far too busy building igloos and breeding dogs to run our sleds. So if you don't like some or all of this rant, what are you going to do, declare war on Canada, invade us and shoot us all? My final parting words...
Take off, eh!

#1596 - SILLY HAT

A few years ago
One of my Aunts
Gave me a toque
For Christmas
It is black
With red devil horns
The responses have been mixed
Once when I was wearing it
One woman called me
"Satan's helper" and an "infidel"
I have to say that
If your faith is that put off
By a silly hat
Then obviously your faith
Is not very strong
By the way,
Just for your information
I do NOT believe in any
Prophets, messiahs, gods, devils,
Heavens or hells And I am quite comfortable
With my life
So, to quote Hank Williams Sr. "Mind your own business"
Because it is just a silly hat.

Full Definition of "DERIVATIVE" From The Merriam-Webster Dictionary

1: a word formed by derivation

2: something derived

3: the limit of the ratio of the change in a function to the corresponding change in its independent variable as the latter change approaches zero 4: a : a chemical substance related structurally to another substance and theoretically derivable from it b : a substance that can be made from another substance

5: a contract or security that derives its value from that of an underlying asset (as another security) or from the value of a rate (as of interest or currency exchange) or index of asset value (as a stock index)

NOMEANSNO APRIL 6TH, 1994 AT THE POLISH HALL

Sometime in late 1993 or early 1994 I signed a contract with Nomeansno's management to be the promoter of a Nomeansno show with The Imagineers & The Naked and The Dead opening. I might have received a good word as a promoter from Tom Holliston of Nomeansno because of a successful show I put on for his other band, The Show Business Giants a year earlier.

Regardless, I did all of the running around and sold enough tickets to cover my expenses, the Nomeansno guarantee and a few hundred dollars for an emergency. A few weeks into March the tickets all sold out and because I didn't print any more tickets I pissed off a couple of the record stores that were selling tickets. My logic for being a promoter was to make Nomeansno as much money as possible and the best way to do that is to let the tickets sell out and then have people pay at the door. That way Nomeansno would make a bunch more money because of their small guarantee (covered with ticket sales) and their percentage of the door sales. Door sales were $2 more than the ticket cost.

On a side note, this was the first show that I put on that I paid myself. Nomeansno's booking agent thought that to be a promoter and not pay yourself was ridiculous so they paid me $100 to do the show! I mainly did shows to help friends' bands out and didn't take anything extra besides my expenses.

The night of the show was intense, I figured that 400 or 500 tops would attend (the biggest show I did prior to Nomeansno drew about 300) but just over 700 attended! I remember K.H. midway through The Imagineers (K.H. and A.H. always did my doors) come running up to me in a panic telling me, "Corey, Corey, Corey! You have to do something! We have over $5000 in cash!" Right then I figured that I was in over my head.

At another point in the show a furious young mother came up to me angry because I didn't allow stage diving at my shows, I NEVER allowed stage diving at my shows and she was angry because her son wanted to do his first stage dive. I asked her if her son put a foot through a monitor, then would she pay for the damages? Or if her son put a mic through Rob Wright's teeth then would she pay for his dental work? She called me a motherfucking asshole and stormed off. It was definitely foolish on my part, but I never bought insurance, which if something happened and I had no insurance I would have been in a great deal of hot water.

Because of all the drama at the show, I only got to watch one Naked and The Dead song, one Imagineers song and not a single note of Nomeansno. Bummer! At the end of the show Rob Wright of Nomeansno and I counted the money in a broom closet off the side of the stage and Rob was nice enough to pay me an extra $100!

When I said that this was the first time that I was paid for a show I promoted, it wasn't entirely honest because at the end of EVERY show I put on, big or small hall, I ALWAYS swept the floors by myself. My helpers thought that I was an idiot. Little did they know that I swept the floors all by myself because after the show had ended, there was so much loose money on the floors it made it totally worth it for me to sweep. Especially The Polish Hall because of its size I swept up over $60 of loose money! The Polish Hall was the biggest hall I had ever used. I think that it holds about 600 but I could be wrong, so getting just over 700 was dangerous to say the least.

A few months after the Nomenano show I had a Jello Biafra spoken word show scheduled at The Garneau Theatre. Unfortunately it was canceled because Jello suffered a leg injury that prevented him from standing for a while. So soon after Nomeansno I decided that four years of being a promoter was quite enough drama and I quit promoting for good, other than Nomeansno, Forbidden Dimension, The Loved One, Pal Joey and a few other bands, because most of the time I felt like a glorified babysitter. So after 4 years I quit and the fun was over. Besides meeting the bands and helping them out, I don't miss being a promoter one bit.